Dominion Oluyadi

YOU' RE NOT INFERIOR

Dominion Oluyadi

YOU' RE NOT INFERIOR

...mental reposition of youth!

Blessed Hope Publishing

Imprint

Cover image: www.ingimage.com

Publisher:
Blessed Hope Publishing
is a trademark of
International Book Market Service Ltd., member of OmniScriptum Publishing Group
17 Meldrum Street, Beau Bassin 71504, Mauritius
Printed at: see last page
ISBN: 978-613-7-89302-9

YOU'RE
NOT
INFERIOR
...mental reposition of youths!
Dominion Oluyadi

YOU'RE

NOT

INFERIOR

YOU'RE NOT INFERIOR is published by **Eagles Publication International** [The publishing arm of Corporate Character Dev.& Mgt. Sch. RC.1535149].

Suite 31, LordReigns plaza, 162, Ipaja Road, Opp. Anchor University - Lagos. +234[0]9037205205.

www.worldgreatestcharacter.org

drdominionoluyadi@gmail.com

ACKNOWLEDGEMENT

YOU'RE NOT INFERIOR is not a product of educational backlog, human wisdom, academic intelligence - or motivational projection.

This recipe is 100% a product of **God's direct inspiration and passion geared towards the urgent - rescue mission of teenagers and youths** from juvenile delinquency, ravaging the world!

The author is just a human tool chosen for this assignment [by virtue of his personal availability].

CONTENTS

INTRODUCTION

We are living in a digital age. The global circulation of the information technology and other information – dissemination devices has made it possible for every minor information extracted from human ideologies go virile in few seconds by a fingertip!

Information technology reality does possess it's good sides and bad sides. Digital space makes it possible for the western folks – youths especially, to upload their [digitally] packaged their ideologies via pictorial-graphics, in such way that it appears to be real, meanwhile ninety percent of such presentations are not!

On the contrary, accessibility to such pictorial-graphics oriented magic cum social media manipulations to a large extent sort of place the average African youth in a wrong frame of mind. Living such with a perspective that Africans are inferior to other whites' folks. Worse in support of such illusion is orchestrated by the mismanagement of African-continent's resources, by her leaders, who predominantly loot the treasuries as each government take their turn to lead, with major target to [intentionally], ground their economies through corruption.

You're not inferior was created to immediately; withdraw, dissuade and destroy such mental relegation ideology, infused into our youths for several generations now – by helping each one see realities in human-equality, irrespective of color, race, gender, creed, etc.

Chapter 1

Topic: **DO YOU HAVE BRAIN**

How will you feel if your bosom friend should ask you the above question - do you have brain?

The fact is we all have our individual opinion in every issue or matter that transpires before us. We have different ears in trying words and thoughts. However, the bottom, line is - what's your take on the issue here? What will be your personal response, if the above question is directed at you, without any adequate preparation, presumption or permutation as regards the subject matter?

The fact down here must, not be treated with levity. The weight of the question carries a great gravity that calls for meditation, critical analyses and rational review.

As long as the book centers on the juvenile, I am appealing to the mind of each teenager and youth to take this question seriously. In fact, I advise you take the question **"do you have a brain"** as a challenging puzzle that is capable of fetching you an academic scholarship or national recommendation which possesses inherent international recognition and other values, even at your juvenile period in life, among your age categories and academic contemporaries around the world. Moreover, to neglect this challenging question is to also further relegate your mental capacity to the normal, common - youth's mental status- quo! A thought that rather believe -what will be will be!

To become special in life, you must be prepared to do abnormal things, because it takes a degree of special mental-ability to enjoy special immunity in the society. The normal thinking will only fetch normal results but [abnormal] radical, analytical - fact-finding thinking will shoot you beyond the skies and stars.

This sort of question ought to challenge your juvenile credibility to withstand whatever is out to play down on your mental dignity and juvenile ability to unravel the intelligence hidden behind the test thrown at you, but now and forever!

Chapter 2

Topic: WHAT'S IN YOUR BRAIN

The title of today's lecture may sound similar to the first. Nevertheless, this rather sound more of a probing question than that of the first, which was a challenging one.

Let me help with the breakdown of the above title.

The simplicity of the question is asking after **your brain contents**! In other words, the following question should help you unravel the realities inherent your personal brain-contents.

Now let me help you understand the question better. For instance, whenever you pick up a novel. Flip over the introduction page, or preface. The next page normally reads; "table of contents".

The table of contents literately unveils the contents of the book by virtue of each chapter's heading or title. In other words, the table of contents is the first insight you require to access the full book. It is from the table of contents of each chapter you can imagine the nature, structure and direction of such in terms of overall information inherent the literature. One other information the table of contents does for you is - it affords you with the liberty of the choice to pick on the chapter you desire to read before others. This time you are not constrain or tied to following the table of contents according to it's sequential order. You may decide to read chapter four before reading chapter one, etc.

In the same vein, I want you list out your personal brain contents with brevity.

In other words, "what service can your brain offer the world"?

Here is another example:

My Personal Brain Contents

- I am a thought developer
- I write books for myself
- I write books for people/organisations
- I do proofreading service
- I offer lectures on business/ leadership
- I offer lectures on juvenile/leadership character
- I develop resource materials for conferences, etc.

From the above example you should be able to understand what I mean by the question that serves as the topic for this chapter- **what is in your brain**!!!

To a large extent, the functionality of a product is best described by the end user, and not just the manufacturer who intend to convince the user. You should be able to identify your abilities and special abilities than anyone else.

What is in your brain unveils your personal ability to define your identity with brevity and confidence. You can be called upon to say what you're capable of doing with little or without supervision, this is how many youths have gained prominence. **Understanding and development of personal talent into special ability opens door for unexpected opportunity** - yet, to experience such - you must live ready! The difference between getting ready and living ready is:

- Those who get ready = unprepared folks
- Those who live ready = fully prepared folks

The fact about life reality is; the world is looking for those who are already prepared - hence no one has the luxury of time to waste, by waiting for those who are just getting prepared. Apparently - if you're not prepared you won't also be preferred. The world is on a fast lane, only the prepared are permitted to drive along such space [to avoid accidents].

chapter3

Topic: **PERSONAL BRAIN CONTENT**

I believe from the last chapter you must have understood the treasures inherent your personal brain [contents]?

Your assignment in this chapter is quite simple.

Cut out a blank paper, or draw a graph on your PC with the title in accordance with the above topic.

Make a project of it. Take your time to itemize what you believe your brain can do, or the service you know yourself can render to humanity. You may not need to end the documentation or itemization at a go, but you just open up the page and pay attention to what you document in there.

You can also duplicate such documentation, by placing the compilation on your personal room door, bathroom door, library shelve frame, etc, a place you know is conspicuous enough for you to observe it as you go on daily - you must be serious with this project. Believe me for the first time this new measure will help you do self-mental evaluation. This exercise is bound to further reinforce your personal discipline by focusing on developing your mentality and juvenile capacity.

Such assignment will help you place value on your life by the unique value you place on each moment and time you spend in "your entire lifetime!"

Chapter 4

Topic: ***YOU HAVE A BRAIN***

At this junction, it is necessary for us to consult the expert on brain study, for correct/current information and further, relevant education.

Each time one, or people allow the professionals to handle issues that requires professionalism, the best of information and knowledge surrounding such will always be unveiled without any ado, because, facts will be made available without struggle.

You cannot think or assume you could conclude on brain matter without consulting a neurosurgeon just as you cannot conclude on childbearing subject without involving the gynaecologist – in the same vein – a professional neurosurgeon must be brought on board to widen our horizon on the human brain and the topic in focus!

The next portion of this chapter is as documented by **Ben Carson, MD – A very popular black American Neurosurgeon, who has operated on thousands of brains successfully:**

- *"Inside each human brain are approximately 86 billion neurons interconnected by more than 100 trillion synapses (estimated since no one has counted them all yet), which science has only barely begun to understand.*
- *You brain started developing almost immediately after conception. During the first month of your mother's pregnancy, your body was creating*

neurons at the rate of about 400 million per day.

- *Your brain generates electricity constantly, enough every walking minute to keep a low - wattage light bulb fully lit. So when you say, that's a bright idea, your statement could be literally as well as figuratively true.*
- *Sensory signals move along an alpha motor neuron in your spinal cord at 268 million per hour (mph). This is the fastest transmission of this type in the body. Skin sensory receptors, which travel at about 1 mph, are among the slowest in the body because they do not have myelin sheath, which would insulate them and boost their speed.*
- *The brain of the normal twenty year old human possess 100,000 miles of myelin - covered nerve fibres.*
- *Your brain can feel no pain because it has no pain receptors. The organ that controls the whole nervous system and it cannot feel pain! This is why we can operate on the brain without worrying*

about the pain level of the patient. It's also the reason why we can perform surgery on people who are awake, as they feel absolutely nothing.

- *Harvard university neuroscientist Jeff Lichtman, who is attempting to map the brain, has calculated that several million pet bytes of data storage would be needed to index the entire human brain.*
- *When scientists try to quantify the capacity of the human brain, the number get so high that we can't get our minds around them.* ***The potential of your mind is literally mindboggling.****"*

Culled from; **YOU HAVE A BRAIN [ZONDERVAN .COM]**

Chapter 5

Topic: **MANAGE YOUR BRAIN**

Welcome to day five!

My dear young personality, I know you might be wondering all this while, why on earth; I have been dwelling on the brain topic (after all there are a thousand and one issues affecting the juvenile world], Why brain?

Merriam Webster dictionary defines brain as the organ of the body in the head that connects:

Functions

Movements

Sensations

Thoughts

The ability to think

A very intelligent person

Full definition

The portion of the vertebrate central nervous system enclosed in the skull. And continuous with the spinal cord through the foreman megrim that is composed of neuron and supporting and nutritive structures, (such as glair) and that integrate sensory information from inside and outside the body in controlling autonomic function) such as heart beat and respiration, in coordination and directing correlated of learning.

In a bid to understand the management of your brain, let's consider the following highlight [as boldly written above]:

- Functions
- Movements
- Sensations
- Thoughts

The productive use of the above highlight is what culminates in brain management.

1. If your brain must **function** maximally, then you must engage such in line with what God created it for – "thinking".
2. **Movement** – the movement of your brain changes position from time to time

depending on your thinking pattern, [which must be positive, of course]!

3. **Sensation** – brain sensation is the ability to feel things through your physical senses.
4. **Thought** - thoughts are the processes by which your brain performs usefully, by generating ideas, planning, perceptions, etc. Such activities help your brain experience the process of thinking through issues before drawing conclusion.

In conclusion,

The product of your personal thinking [including your secret thoughts], are practically the realities of your mental investment.

Therefore, when I said manage your brain – I mean to say - manage your mind. I define mind as-

Mental

Investment

Notable

Developments

Your personal line of **mental investment** is what determines notable developments.

Notable development is the hallmark of geniuses - very intelligent people, because they engage their brains (minds) to think, reason, and proffer solutions to the challenges beclouding humanity in different sphere and capacities.

- When you begin to manage your brain (well), as a juvenile today – you're sure of a successful future as you graduate into adulthood.
- When you manage your brain well, you must be up reading, while others are sleeping.
- When you manage your brain well – you're bound to become one of the solution generators in your generation!
- When you manage your brain well – you are likely to turn out to be your nation's helper - that makes you a hero!

27

YOU'RE NOT INFERIOR

Here is my question to you: are you prepared to manage your brain well?

Chapter 6

Topic: ***YOUR LIFE'S VISION***

In the first devotion I made mention of vision briefly while talking about **Dream Building** in page 37. [You could get such to know the angle I am driving at].

In the next few days, I will like to write [speak] extensively on vision.

Vision is one of the avenues that help one in productive brain management.

I have, through sincere observation come to understand that **lack of vision is the major reason behind juvenile character deficiencies** around the world.

If you miss the vision of your personal life, you will definitely be pursuing another person's vision.

29 YOU'RE NOT INFERIOR

To lack your own vision is to lack your own future; to lack your own future is to fight for other people's future, unknowingly = failure!

Vision is what you crave for; because in such contains your whole life evolvement from phase to phase. Your life at a certain stage, or at some point receives wings [of the eagle] to fly above your peers who lacks such visionary hype and height.

Every genuine ambassador who is out to represent an organisation, institution or nation must definitely possess a distinctive vision – vision is what gives one the clarity of direction in any given assignment. Without a clear-cut vision, there will always be confusion. Confusion is the reason for error. Compounded errors gradually initiate horror.

It's of utmost importance that every juvenile equip himself/herself with productivity - oriented vision at a very prime age. Such juvenile's life, with visionary mentality & fortification helps one beat down juvenile distractions in life! Accessibility to personal vision for life, at a very early stage, prepares you for leadership even prior to your leadership positioning in life. Such makes you reason beyond your natural age. It develops your mental capacity for proactive thinking.

Chapter 7

Topic: DEFINITION OF VISION

The **ability to see**; sight or eyesight, something that you **imagine** a picture that you see in your **mind**.

Something you see or dream especially as part of a religious supernatural experience.

From the above definition, let us pick on the words painted boldly.

Ability to see

I like this, ability to see! Please understand not we all see. Especially among young peers, you should remember sometimes you people argue about the reality of what you see at times, because you term to see differently.

What do I mean?

Should you all be asked, to describe what you claim to see exactly - you all must definitely come up with different descriptions. The question is why different descriptions; it is because your individual visual ability is different from each other. Our individual observation capacity comes with disparity

More also, if the teacher is to mark your script after each one's submission of his/her description, definitely the grades will not be same except you spy at each other's answer sheet!

The question is what is responsible for each one's experience?

Individual ability to see

We don't have the same visual ability when it comes to visual expression.

Another fact responsible for this is -

There are three types of eyes

- The eyes that looks
- The eyes that sees
- The eyes that sees clearer

Capacity to see, clearer, varies from person to person. Hence we can't all have or run the same vision in life. A true ambassador cannot be experiencing impaired vision and still expect to perform maximally. Impaired vision degenerates into frustration, because it reduces the productivity and capacities of the affected fellow to minimal achievement when it comes to work appraisal and performance evaluation.

One thing is to be mentally loaded, yet physically limited or relegated sort of, because of impaired vision impediment.

Impaired vision will not become your lot in life!

Chapter 8

Topic: DEFINITION OF VISION [2]

Here is the second reason, which determines the expression of what you claim to see - **imagination.**

Imagination is the formation of mental picture on your mind. What does it imply?

Those who **look** are in the category of those who want to **feed their eyes.**

Those who **imagine** are in the category of those who want to **feed their minds**.

Therefore, should you belong to the second group, it means you are seeing beyond your physical eyes could. It also means you are seeing through whatever your eyes looks or sees per time!

DREAM

Because I have written a bit on dream in the first juvenile character devotional, I will not want to dwell on it here, so I will not be repeating myself.

I am going to provide you with the dictionary definition only:

"Series of the thoughts, vision or seeking that happen during sleep

An idea that is created in your imagination.

Something that, you have waited very much to do, be or have for a long time."

Supernatural experience

The summary of the above; boils down to God showing you certain, yet unknown things! Anything supernatural means - something that is not natural something divine. For instance;
Human being is natural
God is supernatural [Spirit being].

Ambition may come naturally, based on one's frequent thought line or followership addiction to a certain role model in one of the societies of the world. But vision, is contrary to ambition, because vision is orchestrated by God - human creator, hence vision is supernatural in terms accessibility and reality.

Another truth is you can give yourself ambition but you can't give yourself vision - only God gives us

Chapter 9

Topic: **WHAT IS VISION**

I have been able to break down Merriam Webster dictionary definition for you. Now permit me to define vision for you in applicable way.

Short story on vision

A little girl was on a cruise ship, she and her dad were standing on the deck. The day was beautiful and clear. The sky above was clear enough for everyone's visual clarity.

Nevertheless, this little girl was said to stand upon her feet, yet she could not see far off. Then, the dad lifted her up on his shoulders, after a short while she exclaimed in excitement.

"Daddy, I can see farther beyond my eyes can look"

I define vision as follows -

- Vision is the ability to see beyond what the eyes can look
- Vision is the accessibility to the future, today
- Vision is breaking the barrier of limitation from human visualisation.
- Vision is the ability to capture your personal future from a single picture
- Vision comprehends your personal purpose – description with distinction
- Vision is ability to grasp your personal destination in life with precision

- Vision is supernatural accessibility to your destiny details with clarity of understanding.
- Vision is the revelation of your supernatural identity in humanity
- Vision is the blue print of your life details in clear print.
- Vision is having a sure direction without confusion
- Vision is the authencity of your personality in humanity

To understand the details from the above highlights then you need to go over such once or twice, to sift out detailed information inherent the contents.

Chapter 10

Topic: DO I NEED VISION

Today's devotional resource opens up with the question; "Do I need vision?"

Yes! You truly need vision!

One of the reasons for juvenile delinquency in the world today is because about 90% of teenagers and youths lack direction for their lives!

Just like the young girl, whose father lifted up above himself and everyone on the ship deck, she was able to see farther, than her physical eyes could - you cannot see your tomorrow today and still allow yourself to be short sighted.

In the next few days, I will be telling you simple reasons why you need vision.

I promise you, - it won't be boring.

I am all out to work on your brain in this edition. Once your brain is able to grasp the picture I will be showing to you, you're sure to experience a great future. **Knowing what you need helps you discard what you don't - promptly!**

Chapter 11

Topic: VISION UNVEILS YOUR IDENTITY

I am going to put you on a horse race from today's lecture

Baby lion story

YOU'RE NOT INFERIOR

There was a story I learnt as narrated to Dr. Myles Munroe [of blessed memory], a community head equally told it him.

It was about a baby lion that was picked up by one of the old hunters in the community - in one of such hunting spree. He brought home the baby lion after he was sure the mother wasn't coming for him, or anywhere near the scene.

The baby lion was integrated into the sheepfold. After few days he began to blend with sheep's character, he ate their kind of food, played their kind of game and did things in common with his new sheep-family [though, originally he wasn't one; but life is where you find it].

Occasionally, while he was in the company of the sheep each time they are out to grace. After gracing, they retire to a certain riverbank where they normally drink water. Frightening enough, there was this big lion which sometimes roar from across side of the river. Just as you know there is no sheep nor animal that is not threatened at the roar of the lion. Especially when the lion roar- they sheep took to their heels, it was a survival of the fittest experience.

There came a day, the baby lion was the first to outrun the sheep siblings to the river, surprising to the young lion on arrival at the riverbank. As he overlaps the water to drink, he saw the image of himself on the water and it looks exactly like that of the big lion. Then he paused for a while because he was a bit puzzled. He was of the opinion it must have been the big lion. Nonetheless, he drank along with the sheep siblings on their arrival few seconds later. Yet, he was pondering upon the picture he saw prior to his sheep-siblings arrival.

Few weeks later, they were at the riverbank and the big lion roared as usual. While others took to their heels - he boldly swam across, even though his attitude was just like that of the sheep where he was adopted – his physical and outward appearance was that of a lion. However, the big lion did not hurt but gave him warm welcome. As the big lion, turns away from the water bank and head towards the forest. He waited a while, wondering and gazing at the young lion, as he looked behind considering whether to follow the big lion or return to his sheep family. Eventually he decided to follow the big lion to start a new life, **having found his identity – a lion!**

REALITY OF IDENTITY

- Identity makes you **original**
- Identity makes you **bold**
- Identity shows you your **class**
- Identity reveals your true **nature**
- Identity helps you discover **purpose**
- Identity repositions your **ideology**
- Identity establishes your true **identity in reality**
- Identity defines your **personality**

Just like the young lion – who now discovered lions crack bones, while sheep feed on grass.

Identity helps you crack bones - solving great task.

- Lions live in the jungle where it's about survival of the fittest, unlike sheep that depends and are at the mercy of humans for survival in life. Survival in life is by taking personal responsibility.

- Lions are at liberty to hunt whatever animal at whatever time of the day – sheep have no liberty they don't have their own mind or either could make any meaningful decision
- Lions we are told, lives longer than sheep's - why humans are free to hunt down the sheep anytime and anyhow. Have you heard of where lions are hunted down [in a community] without resistance?

Here is the question:
From the above context, which of the animals will you rather chose to become if you were created an animal?
What's your choice among the two, that you believe your identity is going to be in life?

Chapter 12

Topic: VISION DICTATES YOUR DIRECTION

Have you ever read or heard of a ship's survival in a stormy weather [on the sea], without a rudder?

Did anyone ever told you an airplane survived after losing communication synergy - with the control tower?

In the same vein, you cannot successfully develop on your juvenile character adventure, successfully without a specialized direction in life. To develop a specialize direction in life, just like the ship and aeroplane; you will always require vision. Vision is the compass of destiny.

For instance, imagine you're on board a chattered vehicle and the driver ask about the direction of the journey so he could set up the GPS, but You're saying - I don't know?

Or, let's say you are on board a chattered cab, and you immediately gave the driver the address to where you're heading, only for you to begin to hear the GPS announcer mention a route contrary to your designated destination. You're or likely to find yourself in a wrong location at the end of such journey, should you continue on such trip.

Nevertheless, when the right direction is programmed into goggle map, the programmed-announcer is bound to mention names and places it's familiar with based on the direction you programme into it.

Companions of programmed direction

For every addressed direction - the following companions are immediately factored in:

- Definition
- Attention
- Observation
- Clarification
- Destination

With such sequence in place, your confidence is aroused.

Chapter 13

Topic: ***BUYERS & SELLERS WORLD***

In case, you are wondering what the correlation between businesses and character is - I am just trying to open your eyes to the reality of business availability in our society and how it could further arouse your mental reasoning productively.

We are living in a world that is a cohabitation of buyers and sellers. No one survives in the world without buying or selling.

Sellers dictate the prices of commodities. Buyers purchase based on decision of sellers, which comprises of type of commodities etc. For instance, look around you, the vehicles, telecommunication, phone accessories, electrical appliances, domestic utensils, etc.

First, which one of these is manufactured in Africa? We all buyer and sell. Nevertheless, the buyers are at the mercy of sellers.

Only sellers dictate what is sold, the amount it's sold, who to sell to and location for sale per time.

The buyers have lesser choice or control over this fact. Here is wisdom; sellers become richer, while buyers become poorer. Whatever you buy reduces your bank account balance. In addition, whatever you sell [should you be among sellers], increases your account balance.

My observation is – if you're not among the sellers, you're bound to end up poor. I have experimented what I am teaching you. A certain year, I was paid a million naira as fee for sealing a deal. I began to withdraw the money bit by bit. Few months after I became broke, why? Because I was only buying, I was not selling! Continual withdrawal without savings reduces income.

Each time a business transaction takes place anywhere around the world - the seller benefits more, for the account balance of seller increases at the detriment of that of the buyer [which reduces].

What sense am I making here? My dear youngster, if you don't have what you are selling, you will become poor.

This is why you must use your brain. You may be living on your parents or other people's purses today, such opportunities will never last forever.

Nevertheless, while such opportunities persist, you must wake up now! Using your brain helps you focus more on your studies and academic pursuits with addiction - such addiction helps you avoid the plaque called: distraction, which is common with teenager and youth. Moreover, true ambassadors are known to be more dedicated to the course or core business of the organisation they represent per time.

Chapter 14

TOPIC: 4 D'S OF AN IDEOLOGIST

A wise man once said and I believe, he said – "Ideas rule the world"

Everything about the world is ideological. The earth is first, God's personal ideology; nevertheless, every other additional development that makes the earth a comfortable space to occupy is all about ideology.

What you and I make use of daily, such as; telecommunication, electricity, transportation, clothes, internet, technology, etc are products of human ideological thinking.

I have said often that - **every idea, generated from one part of the world is a proof there is already a need for such idea in another part of the world.**

This is why, even as a juvenile ambassador, part of your responsibilities as representative of any organization is to be ideological in your thinking. Moreover, as you navigate through the journey of destiny and become well informed and inclined with your personal earthly responsibilities - you will also do well to observe the following structure in the course of your growth.

DISCOVER

Every idea begins as a discovery. Every product enjoyed by humanity today started ass discovery by certain individual yesterday. Humans have unlimited potential for inventions and innovations that are capable of proffering varied solutions to human urgent situation - yet such ideology usually begins as discovery.

Discovery of every idea begins as **perception**

DEVELOP

I believe you must have heard of the man who created the electric bulb, **Thomas Edison** – and how he fought all through while developing the idea over 999 times before success was achieved.

Development of ideas consist of **observation, conception** and **interpretation**

Chapter 15

TOPIC: **4 D'S OF AN IDEOLOGIST [2]**

DOCUMENT

This is where many fail - documentation!

I heard of two pastors who were best of friends from their youth.

Both pastors were full of different ideas by virtue of books they were privileged to read, and the sort of education acquired.

However, there was a major disparity among both. One got used to documenting his thoughts and ideas on papers and also saving such. On the contrary, the other pastor was only known for sharing his thoughts and ideas of greatness without documentation. Several years later, opportunities began to call out for them. Before you know it, the pastor who documented his thoughts and ideas turned such information into books and audio tapes, and such, which went virile. Not too long he emerged a prominent personality around the world because of documentation of his thoughts and ideas even when it was a humble beginning. After a while, the relationship between both pastors collapsed.

One began soaring as eagle while the other crawled like turtle!

Come to think of it; what do you think the world could look like assuming there are no books to read?

I saw in one of the ancient books that God is not just a thinker but also a writer!

Great leaders think on paper! Documented thoughts last longer in the information world than mere declaration.

DISTRIBUTION

Here is the last of the four- distribution!

Don't forget, I said in the last conversation, how the pastor's resource materials began to go virile, which later culminated into his success?

Documents are normally meant to be distributed! It doesn't matter how long a document is kept safe, once it lacks the opportunity for distribution, such inherent information and content will end up in illusion.

Documents are simply information in written form -information stored up safely, waiting for the right dispensation for human consumption through appropriate dissemination channels.

Chapter 16

TOPIC: WHO'S INFLUENCING YOU

This topic is very crucial to every juvenile personal character development, attainment and sustenance. You may be thinking it does not matter but it does. We all grow up under different influence per time.

Whatever you buy-in into influences you directly or indirectly- there is no assumption about this fact. The movie stars, singers, fashion models, television stars, teachers, bloggers, pastors, etc., each has a direct mental synergy with yours – with or without your consent.

The fact is, man cannot actually develop from stage to stage outside of influence, especially, in the area of mental development - it will always require influence. Without a certain degree of influence on each class session, a teacher will always find it difficult to impact on the student, his level of intelligence – academically - notwithstanding! Such may not be able to convince the student on a particular subject or thought line; even though the student will require such information to thrive in a chosen course of his. To create impact, maintain dignity, and sustain subsequent influence over the present or generations coming you must pay attention to your influencer make up today. The best part of any man's life and existence is that of his youthful age years. There are certain things that will require God's ultimate intervention to repair – should a youth play down on such vitalities during juvenile phase in life.

I mean you will do so well to investigate your influencers in order to ascertain why they influence you and why you should continuously remain under such influence. Every success or failure story you hear about people around the world has largely, inputs from influence!

Chapter 17

TOPIC: INFLUENCERS' INVESTIGATION

Every human being, great or small, learned or unlearned, civilized or primitive, rich or poor, black or white, etc. has someone out here (known or unknown) who influences him/her (positively or negatively).

For instance, naturally speaking, children are normally products of their parents /teachers' influence.

The order placed and rules set in each family or institution directly bothers on children. Therefore, the issue of choice do not come in here. Because these set of adults are the ones, the children are required to sit under, daily, at least five days a week. Judging by what experts says; that whatever one does for 21-28 days at a stretch becomes one's habit. Habits determine our peculiarities, our constant peculiarities dictate our behaviour - consistent behaviour defines our human character: such is the brevity of the power of influence!

WISDOM

Now, here comes wisdom. Definitely, you as a person with any iota of doubt, is aware that you certainly have the stronghold of influence that hold sway over your life; is that correct?

Take another step further by writing down your sorts of influence and from whom each has gained control over your life.

I repeat.

- Step one - what sorts of influence
- Step two - who are the influencers
- Step three – what are the benefits / losses
- Step four – commence investigation
- Step five – what are the contents of the character of your influencers' each
- Step six - what are the values your influencers prioritise mostly
- Step seven - what does each individual pedigrees looks like, in terms of general life overview.

Note:

This assignment may take time but you must make project of it, in other to ascertain if you should stop following whom and why?

For instance, **when you come on twitter, there are already lots of those to follow- you don't just follow anyone until you have ascertain who to follow and why you want to follow and why you want to follow such individual or organization after you have investigated the pedigree of such.**

In the same vein, your personal character driven life cycle may not be completed or successful, until you have thoroughly investigated your influence.

Chapter 18

Topic: THE PLACE OF TALENT

I tried to close this book outside of this chapter- yet, I see myself coming back to it at last.

Talent is; a special ability that allows someone to do something well - Merriam Webster.

My dear youngster, you must understand everyone and every human and animals

specie created by God was inherently infused in with special ability.
For instance, fishes will never learn or struggle to swim - neither will birds attend aeronautical institute before flying. Both fishes and birds are species created with individual inherent ability to swim and fly accordingly.

In the same vein, human beings - we were created with inherent talents and special abilities!
Mind you, talent is not education, you can use your education to support talent, but you cannot use education to manufacture talent. If you should ask me, I will tell you talent is superior to education.

Purpose

The purpose of talent is to solve a minimum of one problematic situation. When you develop your talent enough, you will solve more problems.

Riches

Talent is given to man as gift, in other to convert the availability of such into serving humanity. In the continuity of such service – genuine riches are acquired. Have you noticed many singers and film artistes have become very rich by engaging their talents, including, comedians, especially in the 21st century?

Values

The value you put into your talent determines the value people place on your personality - via talent. It is only when it comes to talent that the scale of charges is relegated because each one decides what he or she paid as service charges in exchange for rendering service to mankind [via talent usage].

Personal authority

You have personal authority over your talent. You decide what you charge as fee per time.

I learnt some African singers charges as much as N10,000,000 (ten million naira) for a single show.

Chapter 19

Topic: THE PLACE OF TALENT [2]

Recently, I was told **Anthony Joshua** received over N30 billion naira for defeating his opposing boxer! How many professors have you heard receive such whooping amount in exchange for their educational services – in their lifetime?

Education is the acquisition of human knowledge in relation to discoveries embedded in nature and science. On the contrary, **talent is the natural inbuilt software by God into each human being and for the holistic well being of humanity – in different capacity**!

In the month of December 2019

I wrote two books for a woman, a philanthropist and I charged her what I desired as fees - because I have the sole authority to use my talent appropriately.

Positive

Nevertheless, our individual talent is supposed to be engaged, positively. Every destruction-oriented talent and skill, contributing negative effects on the world around is condemned. In addition, as such, negative talents and gifting do not normally last long!

You must ensure your talent enriches the earth by alleviating the suffering of humanity, nothing outside of this – is of God!

What is your talent?

In closing this chapter, I couldn't forget, not all teenagers and youths recognize they have talents. The following tips will definitely help in the assessment of your personal talent.

- Create time to think about yourself in an isolated place, possibly your bedroom, a convenient place where you're free from interruption from friends, family, music, screen, phone, etc.
- Observe the following with honesty

-What have I been doing well

-What can I do without little or no supervision?

-What problem do I think I can solve for others, perfectly.

-What am I good at without any primary learning from anyone?

-What do people commend me for doing, especially each time I do such!
-What is the place of my passion? Something I can spend hours on or in without minding if I have eaten or not!
-Which of the subjects am I good at, in school – why am I good in such (than others)?
-What am I always prepared to do for people without asking for charges or payment?
-What do I do better than others do among my school peers or groups, etc.
-What pattern of life do I want to lead or create as a new trend, which people are yet to see, notice or commenced?
-What is it that gives me much more joy, each time I am rendering such service, activity, etc.
Think back on your life so far, consider your skills, gifting, traits, natural abilities, frequent activities, things of interests, personal values, etc.
Write out your voluntary charity gestures.

What about you're thought line about career you once considered favourable – if opportunity knocks your door.

Ask your friend to tell you what and where they also notice your skills lie.
You can equally suggest it to your parents or guardians, especially the ones you're in good tune with.

Pray

Pray to your creator for direction and inspiration. Because this rather helps many people, I believe it will help in your case too. God is a universal God, He understands all religions, including yours and He is ever willing to answer those whose request comes with sincerity and seriousness!

Observation/sensitivity

In conclusion, it's not enough to carry out the above exercise from time to time. Nevertheless, it is more important for you to observe. You must be sensitive enough to access the answers to the above questions all by yourself.

I am waiting for the day the world will celebrate your talent with a loud ovation, in the shortest term. Congratulations!!!

Chapter 20

Topic: THE PLACE OF CHARACTER

In the course of my administration of training for leaders and juvenile, I have observed very few youths are able to survive at the top when they become famous or successful.

Charisma may introduce you, but it will take a great degree of personal character for you to be sustained, at the top of whatever career you find yourself in life. The limit of your character will determine the height of your placement in life.

- Character is what you think, with no one knowing
- Character is what you do secretly, with no one seeing.
- Character is your attitude when you are offended
- Character, just like the titanic ship builders said, "Even God cannot sink it"; it exposes your weakness - during your pick of enthusiasm.
- Character is the anchor that helps the ship survives any storm – it holds!

- Character clarity determines what sort of weight of challenges you can sustain in life per time.

Two things will help you sustain your true character [that is if you have it]:

- Self-identity – knowing who you are
- Self discipline - fighting to defend who you`re

Chapter 21

Topic: THE EAGLE'S LIFESTYLE

As for me, I see the eagle as birds' ambassador! If you haven't learnt anything about the eagles' lifestyle - you have learnt nothing.

There are quite many secrets, which make up the eagle, and such further distinguishes the eagle uniquely, among its aerial kingdom contemporaries.

Should you have carried out studies on any bird, in addition, if you have not conducted a search on the eagle, then you have not studied anything tangible, knowledgeable, value-added in terms of perspective (on animal's kingdom), etc.

I observed many organizations and nations around the world display the eagle bird as their logo! Such engagement calls for investigation. Until I discovered the untold secrets about the eagle, then such discovery aroused my interest so much that I, have been privileged to author several editions and books - tittles on eagle.

Have you once heard about the eagle bird?

One great difference about the eagle among other birds is – discipline! I am going to mention the character before the end of this chapter, but I need to sensitise you on the eagle's relevance amongst it's contemporaries. The life style of the eagle is a supposed emulation for every teenage or youth's life administration-pattern, and for the few who sincerely aspire to leap above their equals and superiors in whatever chosen field.

To walk in the pattern of the successful and intelligent is to equally end up, becoming intelligent – successful!

Should you insist on investigating my claims, why not search my name - **Dominion Oluyadi** (via amazon.com).

Talking about this edition of The Ambassadors' [Character] Devotional – you must have noticed the cover page design reveals four eagle birds association. It will amount to error should I complete this book without dedicating a chapter to the eagle bird - even though I know most of the principles I adopted in this book are indirectly the way of life of the eagle bird.

Chapter 22

Topic: THE EAGLE'S LIFESTYLE [2]

Eagles' mentality

The eagle's lifestyle here, is embedded in its characteristics and mentality and as follows:

Mentality of the eagles

1. **Identity Mentality**
   The eagle is one bird who understands the wind because of it's personal identity. Such identity helps it maximise the wind, while other birds are struggling with by flying against the wind - instead the eagle glide on its wave by soaring until it gets closer to its destination before spreading the feathers for objective precision reason!
2. **Genetic Security Mentality**
   The eagles understand the relevance of its genes, hence it seldom engages in casual sex until it's genuinely prepared

for marriage. This is also could be possible to be one of the reasons the eagle is uncommon with cross breeding by animal scientists.

3. **Royalty Mentality**

   I also believe the eagle carries a royalty mentality. Looking at the composition of it's beak, talons, though they are made of brass, yet appears like gold. Such is possibly the reason the eagle is, seldom found in the company of other birds often. Your association often dictates if you're going to experience relegation on loud ovation in life. Kings keep company with kings.

4. **Responsibility Mentality**

   One clear fact about the mother eagle among other birds is, it pays more attention to child nursing.

   It also ensures each of the eaglets must be subjected to flight training from the third week to first month of the arrival in the family. Such compulsory training infuses personal responsibility necessity in the young eaglets before they turn adults! Mother eagle action meant to make the eaglet realise – "eagle species survival gravity and continuity is largely dependent on their ability to fly for life."

5. **Loyalty Mentality**
   The eagle is loyal in its dealings. The eagle's loyalty conscience and consciousness will not permit it to feast on its prey after being married. Not until the prey is brought home for family feast, except the prey become unnecessarily become stubborn, adamant or too large to lift. Such loyalty also helps discipline the eagle against marital infidelity.

Chapter 23

Topic: THE EAGLE'S LIFESTYLE [3]

6. **Self-Recreation Mentality**

   This is the final disposition of the eagle's mentality series.

   Eagle's potentially lives up to 70years before final death, but at age 30, the eagle's begin to notice diminishing return on its body system.

   Such affects:

   - Beak - Mouth
   - Talons - Fingers
   - Feathers - Arms

Such weakened experience affects the creativity and productivity identity of the eagle, thereby making the eagle vulnerable to its environment and wild life space.

Self-Recreation Exercise

The eagle, undergo a self-recreation by subjecting itself to brutality.

Having separated itself to the mountain, for different surgical operation purposes

The eagle begins to pull the **talons** [fingers] from it's root until it ensures all fingers are destroyed totally.

After a month or so when the talons begins to grow out fresh ones, the eagle begins to knock it's **beak** [mouth] against the rock, and this it does continuously until the beak is totally shattered eventually.

After another one-month plus, when the beak begins to grow out new ones, the eagle picks on the **feathers** - ensuring every feather is uprooted until it becomes featherless!

After another one month plus, the feathers begins to grow out fresh brand new feathers. All different stages of surgeries will last for between four to five months or more, depending on individual eagle and the processes and healing duration.

Lesson

My dear eaglet, here is the lesson I'll like you to observe in the eagle's recreation surgeries.

- The recreation of the eagle's **beak** symbolises the necessity of **personal mental productivity/holistic recreation**
- The recreation of the eagle's **talons** symbolises the recreation of **personal talents and skills.**
- The recreation of the eagle's **feathers** symbolises the necessity of **personal rebrand [packaging] of general lifestyle and character!**

If this chapter is the only knowledge you're going to take and yield yourself [to its demands], in the whole chapters of this devotional - I assure you of greatness in life!

Chapter 24

TOPIC: 4 D'S OF AN IDEOLOGIST

A wise man once said and I believe, he said – "Ideas rule the world"

Everything about the world is ideological. The earth is first, God's personal ideology; nevertheless, every other additional development that makes the earth a comfortable space to occupy is all about ideology.

What you and I make use of daily, such as; telecommunication, electricity, transportation, clothes, internet, technology, etc are products of human ideological thinking.

I have said often that – **every idea, generated from one part of the world is a proof there is**

already a need for such idea in another part of the world.

This is why, even as a juvenile ambassador, part of your responsibilities as representative of any organization is to be ideological in your thinking. Moreover, as you navigate through the journey of destiny and become well informed and inclined with your personal earthly responsibilities - you will also do well to observe the following structure in the course of your growth.

DISCOVER

Every idea begins as a discovery. Every product enjoyed by humanity today started ass discovery by certain individual yesterday. Humans have unlimited potential for inventions and innovations that are capable of proffering varied solutions to human urgent situation - yet such ideology usually begins as discovery.

Discovery of every idea begins as **perception**

DEVELOP

I believe you must have heard of the man who created the electric bulb, **Thomas Edison** – and how he fought all through while developing the idea over 999 times before success was achieved.

Development of ideas consist of **observation**, **conception** and **interpretation**

Chapter 25

TOPIC: 4 D'S OF AN IDEOLOGIST [2]

DOCUMENT

This is where many fail - documentation!

I heard of two pastors who were best of friends from their youth.

Both pastors were full of different ideas by virtue of books they were privileged to read, and the sort of education acquired.

However, there was a major disparity among both. One got used to documenting his thoughts and ideas on papers and also saving such. On the contrary, the other pastor was only known for sharing his thoughts and ideas of greatness without documentation. Several years later, opportunities began to call out for them. Before you know it, the pastor who documented his thoughts and ideas turned such information into books and audio tapes, and such, which went virile. Not too long he emerged a prominent personality around the world because of documentation of his thoughts and ideas even when it was a humble beginning. After a while, the relationship between both pastors collapsed.

One began soaring as eagle while the other crawled like turtle!

Come to think of it; what do you think the world could look like assuming there are no books to read?

I saw in one of the ancient books that God is not just a thinker but also a writer!

Great leaders think on paper! Documented thoughts last longer in the information world than mere declaration.

DISTRIBUTION

Here is the last of the four- distribution!

Don't forget, I said in the last conversation, how the pastor's resource materials began to go virile, which later culminated into his success?

Documents are normally meant to be distributed! It doesn't matter how long a document is kept safe, once it lacks the opportunity for distribution, such inherent information and content will end up in illusion.

Documents are simply information in written form -information stored up safely, waiting for the right dispensation for human consumption through appropriate dissemination channels.

Chapter 26

SPIRITUALITY: CHARACTER STRONGHOLD

In my years of research on developing resources and various training materials for character and other roadmap tutorials generation – for leaders, adults, and youths, I discovered the place of spirituality couldn't be relegated neither substituted!

I also discovered the reason for this shortfall is this - there are two forces clamouring for human attention daily: they are forces of GOOD AND EVIL – each one of these forces is always fighting to gain predominant attention of the man. The forces in question influence what we do and why we do what we do - with or without our consent. At times are left to wonder why you do some certain things. You even regret certain actions of yours. Even when you are not able to show such or accept responsibility for such flaw, openly or publicly – yet in your secret place, you're left n he euphoria of your guilt. Unfortunately, you see yourself repeating the same error over and over. After a while such error-like lifestyle then becomes a norm! My dear, this is not really your fault – it's the fault of the particular force responsible for your character shortfall and juvenile delinquencies!

However, should you be interested and you may want to know why? Let me explain this hidden mystery about human composition, which is hidden to scientists.

Reality is - Man is a triune nature.

Man is a spirit.

Man has a soul.

Man lives in a body.

The purpose of the spirit is so that man could relate with God, because God is a Spirit. Spirit communicates with spirits with flexibility. Human communicate with humans with flexibility, through the body and the body serves other bodily exercises, etc. The soul of man is the seat of intellect, thoughts, decisions, etc. The sensitivity of man's spirit to God's voice is what helps man's sensitivity to God's instructions. Observation and prompt adherence to such instructions are the hidden secret to avoidance of errors and horrors. Apparently, God has already set laws to govern the earth. The greatest of such law is known as **the law of cause and effect.** To fault such law is to face the consequences, personal ignorance of such laws' availability is not an excuse for escape – religion has nothing to do with it, because there is no exception to the rule!

Nevertheless, ability to hear God's voice with distinctive clarity is the greatest asset required by man for successful direction and positive guidance capable of offering one expected mental sanity and constant security. **This is why, those who develop their spirit are able to escape hidden temptations that set pace for human; character vulnerability**!

Development

Genuine spiritual development entails:

- Praying
- Fasting
- Scriptural studying
- Meditation, etc.

The above synopses helps us become sensitive to God's voice, because it reduces our carnality by maximising our spirituality, as often as we are able to such – till such becomes a way of life!

Spirituality is the only major source of stronghold, because it possess the inherent capacity to motivate us towards living right and de-motivate from living a wrong – life, because of the God factor who is the epitome of character and character-deity!

Chapter 27

Topic: YOU'RE NOT INFERIOR

The best way to overcome inferiority complex is by thinking superiority thoughts.

We are living in a competitive world no doubt, yet each one will always have a space, if such could understand where his strength lies on time.

Inferiority complex is what usually affects most juvenile, especially when their peers bully, ridicule or relegate them publicly. Here is, in the lecture I want to help you see how you can navigate through it - in this world of competition.

To lack strategic navigation in a world of competition is to end up in - relegation, isolation and frustration!

1. **You're not inferior**

The first step towards overcoming inferiority complex is the ability to understand the fact that – no human being is inferior to other human beings. This is not a statement of consolation but reality.

Biologically speaking, human beings are created alike. For instance, we all equally, have two legs, two hands, one head, two set of eyes, two nostrils, one tongue, etc. Therefore, you must first get rid of such assumption out of your psyche. Whoever told you're inferior is just playing on your personal intelligence. However, what you think about yourself matter the most, than what people think of you. Crush the thought of inferiority so you won't end as mediocrity. Get this fact straight today, and forever – **ambassadors are never inferior set of people, neither is the ambassador of any**

nation inferior to that of another nation – and you are one!

2. **Colour**

When growing up, I used to think the white folks are angels and that they are better or special humans than we blacks – but as I grew into the age of reasoning, I discovered the colour of every human being is because of the climate of the nation where such is born and lives. The whites are white because they are born under cold weather, such as snow, etc. However, we Africans are born into sunny climate – hence we are black.

Therefore, the same body features of the white folks are same for the black folks.

We have the same blood color/contents flowing in our veins, same brain formation, and holistic body composition, etc. Apparently, the reason many Africans bleach their skin is because they are not proud of their continental identity. The color of your skin is not as important as the content of your brain. There are rich blacks and there are poor whites –

what matter most is not our natural color but natural mindset and the sort of attitude with which we live and lead our lives.

Chapter 28

*TOPIC: **YOU'RE NOT INFERIOR [2]***

3. **You're special**

One way also to live above inferiority complex is by understanding that you are, specially and wonderfully created by God! What do I mean – every human being has a unique fingerprint! There is no fingerprint that is inferior to another! Each one is just special and unique. Some peoples' signatures may be forged, but none has ever succeeded in forging the other's fingerprint. You are not an after-thought. You are customized specie. Your human composition is, tailored to soothe your nature. Such special ideology should arouse your mentality – never to feel inferior! You are who you are meant to be - because you have a special solution to a special situation at a special location in this special generation. This is why those in authority must give you a special attention. More importantly, your prompt understanding of this fact should further guide your conversation, association with discretion. Ambassadors are always known to be frontline folks wherever they appear in the world. Please be informed also that every ambassador equally commands special immunity coverage – and so you are, hence you're special!

4. **Special identity**

This is where you need to wake up into reality. You are a product of special identity. Notwithstanding, not until you understand that you have a special identity you may live continually like a nonentity.

For instance, the birds have flexibility in the skies – that's their identity. Fishes have flexibility in water – that's their identity. Realistically speaking, it's expected that each human being ought to discover where his flexibility lies – that is where identity is born. I am not talking about what your parents wants you to be – but more importantly - who God created you to be! If you don't know who you are you will never as well discover what you have – let alone being able to maximize such!

Chapter 29

TOPIC: ***YOU'RE NOT INFERIOR [3]***

5. Special ability

I believe this will also illuminate your thinking better on the subject matter – you're not inferior!

Let's take the scenario of a conference or event centre as the setting. The hall is well arranged before guests' arrival. What makes the hall setting unique are; the chairs arrangement, quality sound proof, lighting effects, rolling-cameras, chilled atmosphere, functional industrial-fans, good microphones and mixers for quality sound projection support. High quality visual – devices, such as mini digital billboard (or TV], etc. With all these appliances in perfect shape - what do you think the show or the event will turn out to be? Excellence of course!

Now, here is the point am trying to make. Each of the above gadgets represents it's manufacturer. Each one is performing a different service from others. Yet they are able to cohabit the event center without friction, rivalry or competition – that is what constituted the excellence recorded from the program at the event centre!

In the same vein, God did not create humans to survive by competition; rather He created us to function via our individual special ability! just like you see each of those gadgets delivered their best by performing different function, so are we to perform maximally in the world, if only we have first discovered our individual identity, ascertain our ability (like the fish and birds) and then concentrate on such until we become experts at such through tireless capacity building!

6. **Build your brain**

However, I may have touched down on different points, but the whole of this devotional is centred on how the ambassador is able build his/her brain - by boosting the knowledge base.

Student's choice

Brain building requires personal responsibility. Brain building is a matter of choice especially among youngsters. Students may be living in the same hostel, under the same school, taught by same set of teachers, supervised under the same curriculum, yet that is never criteria for equal performance.

Teachers' limitation

Student - researchers are usually ahead of mere students, who only rely on the brains of their teachers. The brain of each teacher largely has it's limit in terms of capacity. The normal hustle and bustle of life sometimes place limit on the scope of each teacher's research. Nonetheless, a smart student will only require to get the information from the teacher, firsthand; then build on it. The reason we are having different versions on each identified product, knowledge-based ideology, etc. is because; discoveries will always continue. No human knowledge is an island. Knowledge is never static, irrespective of the field involved. Have you observed – for every invention, there are other versions of such, sometimes with more functions and potential [absent in the first model]. Knowledge is about inventions and innovations.

The reason the African continent is lacking behind is because, our leaders become trapped in their thinking once they get into positions of authority. Such laxity mentality will always place high limit of knowledge gravity – but, you must determine not to add to such backlog of knowledge casualties! This is the reason for this book – **to raise generation of ambassadors worthy of reforming the world, by first; transforming their own**

minds beyond the color of your skin or limitation of your nation's shortfall!

Chapter 30

TOPIC: YOU'RE NOT INFERIOR [4]

7. **Superior knowledge**

Here is the fact of the matter – superior knowledge. What each one of us do with our brains from time is what determine our individual limit in life! Our individual limit in terms of mental capacity (to think] narrowly or variedly, constitute to what further defines our inferiority or superiority in real life appraisal. Remember inputs will always precede output, meaning the lesser your mental input, the lesser your human output. My summary of defining superior mentality is the ability of the student to discover a line of thought, a subject of interest, intellectual discoveries, etc.

Take a step further to discover those leaders who already arrived with solutions on such – begin to follow their thought line by riding on their mental intelligence, and at the same time build on such information until you become well informed on the same subject. Your wealth of information will eventually serve as resource materials to other someday. When this occur you are bound to also become a sought after - this is how geniuses are born!

8. **Self-content**

This is much more important than everything I have told you in these few chapters back - self-content is a paramount tool for every ambassador who must become an epitome of honour in whatever organization, institution or nation such serves per time.

Self-content is the:

- Balancing of your thoughts and actions
- Balancing of your emotional and life realities
- Balancing of your personal ambition and vision

- Balancing of your purpose and your pursuits
- Balancing of your expectations and life temptations
- Balancing of your human function and your reputation, etc.

You just must be contented! I mean be satisfied with your earnings, not because [I mean] you should be satisfied with failure, what I mean is - ensure you earn whatever comes your way genuinely. Earning mentality is handwork mentality. Winning by-all-means is inclusive of crooked means - you won't need that because such perspective is bound to boomerang someday. When such eventually back fire, it will definitely cripple your efforts and jeopardise your achievements by first destroying your reputation!

This is why I said often that – character is superior to skill. **"Skills birth the product but it takes character to sustain the organization!"**

9. Self-impressed

Here is another important aspect that I must not forget to include in your bid to overcome the possibility of being tempted to feel you're inferior.

Self-impression is the ability that makes one happy with oneself, irrespective of what transpires around one's environment. Mind you, quite many issues will likely choke up your joy. You must determine not to be downcast. Once you accept that you're inferior [though you're not, just because you lack certain things or may be your parents are not meeting up in certain standard of life, temporarily -that you thought they should]. Even at then, you must equally understand that life is in phases; hence all families can never be on the same page, or at the same pace. Families are like different seeds. For instance, a farmer who plants maize will always get his harvest before the one who planted orange. In the same vein, the farmer who planted orange will definitely experience harvest before the one who planted perm kernel seed! You can't actually compare your family with others.

Neither should you compare yourself with others. You are like a building that is under construction – you cannot determine a project under construction, it is at the completion stage of the building project that all the beauty becomes pronounced.

Therefore, don't justify your life or family's future with the present situation. Imagine your family ten fifteen years from now [based on your sort of dreams, visions, aspiration, etc].

Refuse to be depressed! Acquainting yourself with stories of those who have made it, with records of accomplishment of humble beginning, you must be enthusiastic. Hang around friends who possess thought of wisdom, intelligence, and not those that, all they think and talk about in life, is focus on flamboyance, celebrities lifestyle, money, fashion in vogue, latest movies and all other peer-group-pressure-mundane ideologies!

Learn to be a source of joy to your immediate family. Excite everyone with the possibility of succeeding in life by your words of hope. It does not matter if you're the youngest or oldest among your siblings. Even if you're the only child of the family, just let your appearance carry aura of joy. This happens when you gradually surround yourself with materials that carry, humorous and enthusiastic virtues.

Believe me, you are star in the making!

Thanks:

Dr. Dominion Oluyadi
Character Embassy
@Character University
www.worldgreatestcharacter.org

TRUMP TOWER
TRUMP
INTERNATIONAL HOTEL
DONALD TRUMP'S
MENTALITY
INTERNATIONAL HOTEL
Dominion Oluyadi

DOMINION OLUYADI
Vol.1
JUVENILE
CHARACTER
DEVOTIONAL
...solution to juvenile deliquency!
(+daily ettiquette)

POLITICAL LEADERS'
CHARACTER
Devotional
...developing next level attitude in politics!
by
Dominion Oluyadi

7 IDENTITY
OF EAGLE'S
MENTALITY
....Soaring via productive mentality
Dominion Oluyadi

The 8 Laws
OF
Widowhood
Provoking Widow's Mentality
Dominion Oluyadi
Available on Amazon.com

MIX
Papier aus verantwortungsvollen Quellen
Paper from responsible sources
FSC® C105338

Printed by Books on Demand GmbH, Norderstedt / Germany